TURNING DATA
INTO DOLLARS & SENSE

Data Integrity – A 21st Century Imperative

*"As Digital Citizens living in a Digital Society, we all have
an unavoidable responsibility to improve the integrity of
our data to preserve our way of life"*

KENNETH R. GRAHAM

ISBN: 978-1-48359-545-0 (print)
ISBN: 978-1-48359-546-7 (ebook)

This Book is dedicated to
My Heavenly Father
Jesus Christ
My Lord and Savior

"I am the Truth, the Light and the Way" - John 14:6

Lord I am a sinner. Thank you for your Love,

Forgiveness, and Mercy.

I love you.

This Book is also dedicated to
My Parents who are in Heaven
Buck & Lonie Graham

"I was never worth much, but I always tried to be as

good as my word." — Buck Graham

Thanks, Mom and Dad, for everything you did and teaching

me about the truth. I love you.

This Book is also dedicated to K2
My Son
Kenneth R. Graham II
Who is my Heavenly Gift and who is my
Eternal Joy

"Dad, you got to believe. I believe in you." — K2 Graham

Thanks, K2, for the joy you bring to me daily and

believing in me.

I love you.

CONTENTS

PREFACE

IN A VERY SHORT PERIOD OF TIME, IF NOT already, you will be able to tell that I am not a gifted author. I am not one of those people who became famous and then wrote a book, as I am sure you have probably never heard of me. Nor am I someone looking to make a million dollars from a best seller; but if that happens, it will be great. I am just another human being on the planet who wants to share his thoughts and experiences in the hopes that America and the world become a better place for the next generation by increasing the integrity of their information.

I have resisted for years, trying not to write this book as I knew how much work it would require. However, an irresistible force would not allow me to run away from this task. Goldie Hawn said, "You often meet your fate on the road you take to avoid it." Time and time again, I was confronted with life circumstances that brought me back to the need to raise the awareness of the importance of information integrity. As I write the preface now, I am confronted with the possibility of being held in contempt of court and jailed for the perceived failure of not paying alimony to my ex-wife. The reality is I have paid the alimony and have documented evidence of that fact, but I am sure that some technology system within the State of Florida's accounting system has a data disorder that is threatening to compromise the quality of my life. I have had many other circumstances where digital recordings of activities in my life have also caused unnecessary pain. So I have surrendered to the powers that compel me to share my experiences through this medium and hope that in doing so it will improve the quality of people's lives.

Working with companies for over twenty five years that were intensely focused on *technology* when *information* was the precious jewel they were in search of, has also led me to share my observations. I believe our nation, and the world for that matter, has been gripped by what I describe as a Delusional Technology Syndrome. This syndrome of exclusively focusing on technology as opposed to information has led to the manifestation of four Digital Data Disorders that I will describe. I will also give real life examples to show the devastating effects that these Digital Data Disorders have caused. These Digital Data Disorders are costing US businesses over a trillion dollars per year, compromising the health of thousands of Americans, and resulting in significant loss in property values.

I will also discuss the prevention of these Digital Data Disorders and characterize the behavior profiles in many organizations that are affected by them. I will outline remedies that can enrich an individual's life, save or make organizations more money, and provide guidelines to avoid Information Integrity Implosions in the twenty-first century. In the Road Ahead Section, I will share how I believe the winners will be defined in the knowledge economy through the pursuit of information excellence, not just the newest, latest and greatest technology. Godspeed, and I hope these words provide some value to you and yours.

INTRODUCTION

THROUGHOUT THE AGES, HUMANS HAVE always detected a need, and then developed a tool that would satisfy that need. In every age, we have taken raw materials and developed processes and tools that would increase a yield and provide benefit as a result of the increased yield. The increased yield would then improve the quality of our lives. Let me give you a couple of examples of how this has worked in the Agricultural and Industrial Ages, and then let's apply this same model to the Information Age.

	Agricultural Age	Industrial Age	Information Age
Raw Material	Natural Resources	Energy	Data
Process	Farming	Manufacturing	Programming
Tools	Oxen/Plow	Machinery	Technology
Yield	Food	Products	Information
Benefit	Increased Survival	Increased Productivity	Increased Knowledge

In the agricultural and industrial ages we focused on the yield, but somehow in the information age we have lost sight of the yield and instead focus on the Tool. The intense focus on technology has created many unintended and unexpected consequences.

Agricultural Age

Agriculture Age

Industrial Age

The detected need in the Information Age is the need to turn data into information and by doing so, increase our knowledge and thus improve the quality of our lives.

Information Age

1. What Data is Required?   2. Process Data Into Information   3. Leverage the Tools

4. Increase Information Yield

5. Improve the Quality of Your Life

As a young boy, I grew up on a farm and saw firsthand how crop yields affected our way of life. Low crop yields decreased the quality of my family's lives. High crop yields, conversely, increased the quality of our lives. Being a young adult, I also experienced the intense focus that was placed on generating high-quality fuels while working with one of the largest oil and gas companies. Higher quality fuels created higher profits. Lower quality fuels had to be refined again, increasing costs and lowering profits.

However, the majority of my experiences have been in the Information Age, and it is rare to hear anyone talk about the information yield out of their multi-million dollar technology systems. Even less spoken of is the benefit the technology system will provide in terms of increased knowledge. We seem to have lost our focus in the Information Age as we spend more time, money, and energy in developing new tools (technology systems) as opposed to focusing on the quality of the yield (Information) and creating high-quality information systems. We never focused more on the tractor than the crop yield on the farm. I am also sure that people in earlier days did not focus most of their energy on the oxen or plow. So my question is why is so much attention placed on hardware, software, networks, phones, etc. as opposed to focusing on the information that is needed to action a decision? This information can increase revenues, contain costs, increase customer satisfaction, provide a better diagnosis, and many other information requirements that an organization or individual may need to prosper. Most organizations today are drowning in data. Data, the raw material, continues to be a raw material after being processed through these multi-million-dollar technology systems, and the information need goes unmet.

This focus on the tools in the Information Age is a condition that I have seen as widespread, and I describe it as Delusional Technology Syndrome (DTS).

Definition: *Delusional Technology Syndrome (DTS)* – A symptomatic condition whereby the focus on technology is so intense that every business opportunity is pursued through technology. There is very little regard to what information is required to maximize the benefit the business opportunity presents.

As a result of the focus on the tool, the business and programming processes have been flawed, creating low-quality information. This has driven the creation of Digital Data Disorders (DDD) throughout the world's technology systems.

Definition: *Digital Data Disorder* **(DDD)** – A data condition whereby the integrity of the information is compromised as a result of a system error, human error, or human intention.

Data, by definition, is the observation we make of our reality. If our recordings of our observations are flawed, then unintended consequences can occur. Given that we live in an age where we are digitally recording our realities at higher and higher levels, I want to speak of my experiences in finding how these digital recordings are consequential and how they continue to erode the quality of all of our lives.

Because we have intensely focused on technology as opposed to the information the technology manipulates and communicates, we are decreasing the quality of our lives. Our intense focus on technology over the last several decades has left the integrity of our information in shambles. Failure to address this imperative has and will continue to compromise the value of our lives and the lives of future generations. The time to clearly understand the impact of information integrity in our lives is now!

We must all understand the subtlety of these Digital Data Disorders and their enormous costs to all

Americans every year. Every organization, small, medium, and large, public or private, nonprofit and profit alike, must meet the challenge of promoting the importance of information integrity. Power, capital, and resource consolidation delivered through technology in and of itself has been detrimental to our way of life. This will continue to be so if we do not address the need for ensuring information has integrity for the benefit of us all, and not for the benefit of the few who control the medium which stores, manipulates and presents information.

An entire system of government, a national economy, and a society of free people that is based upon truth is now being threatened, in large measure because of low levels of information integrity.

Definition: *Information Integrity* - The assurance that the data being managed and accessed is a true record of reality. It has neither been tampered with, nor altered or damaged through system error or human intention.

Information security is not the same thing as information integrity. When some of the first computers were being developed to calculate missile trajectories for the US government, there were two primary concerns. One was information integrity. Because they were using the computer to calculate missile trajectories, they wanted the calculations to be accurate. They wanted to hit the intended target only and not some other unintended target. The second concern was information security. They wanted to secure the information so it would not end up in the wrong hands and compromise the competitive advantage the computer would provide to the United States.

Today, we have the same two primary concerns. Information security garners much attention. Identity theft is the largest growing crime. But information integrity garners very little attention and is often thought of as information security. As a result, the lack of information integrity is costing us thousands of lives, trillions of dollars, and catastrophic loss of property values every year.

If you use, create, or consume information, then you should be aware of the Informational Integrity Imperative for the twenty-first century. This information-centric economy in which we live requires our information to have integrity. Otherwise, it will continue to deteriorate the way of life we treasure for ourselves and our children. Over the last several years, something has been going on in America that has changed our way of life, and most would say not for the better.

The manipulation of perceived realities through technology cannot just be the tool of the few, the powerful, the included, the spinners, the crooks, and the incompetents. The low level of integrity associated with information has necessitated an:

Information Integrity Imperative:

As digital citizens in a digital society, we, the people, have an unavoidable responsibility to increase the integrity of our information to preserve the wellness and wholeness of our way of life in America.

Let me highlight how the lack of information integrity is changing our way of life and not for the better. The national and state election results of 2000, 2002, 2004, 2006, 2008, and 2012 have been subjected to critical analysis that has more than substantiated significant integrity issues with the results of many of them. In the healthcare industry, where life and death decisions are made based upon low integrity information, thousands of people die every year. Even decisions to go to war are made on information that has debatable degrees of integrity; case in point was the Iraq war. In each of these cases, *information integrity* played a role in the events that created very negative outcomes, destroying lives, property, and costing trillions of dollars.

Definition: *Information Integrity Implosion* - A significant breakdown of available trusted information resulting in catastrophic human, property, and monetary damages.

Maybe the most infamous *Information Integrity Implosion* was 9/11, whereby information stored and managed in government agency silos could not be synthesized, analyzed, and actioned to prevent a devastating attack on our nation.

Many research institutions and other reputable sources indicate that low levels of *information integrity* are costing American businesses over a trillion dollars a year. Many believe that numbers could be much larger given our information- centric economy and the lack of focus on the need for high-quality information. This condition has occurred in large measure as a result of not managing information technology in an acceptable manner. Another contributing factor is that information has been subordinated to technology in terms of importance. Ninety-nine percent of our time and money have been focused on managing and acquiring *technology* as opposed to managing and acquiring high-integrity actionable *information*.

As a result, the tipping point has arrived whereby we are forced to focus more on the integrity of information because, traditionally, we have not done so, and the costs have been enormous. Specifically, the labeling, definition, and organization of our information is what must become one of our primary concerns if we are to preserve our way of life that so many people have cherished and sought for generations. The negative effects of deficient *information integrity* on our quality of life has yet to be fully measured or realized. Failure to embrace the *Information Integrity Imperative* will cause us to risk losing the things that have made our nation the greatest nation on earth. In the Great Recession of 2008, experts claim that more than nine trillion dollars of property values were destroyed, most of which was caused by a lack of information integrity in mortgage banking systems. Personal greed facilitated not by information systems but by technology systems afflicted with Digital Data Disorders also played a key role in the worst recession since the Great Depression. (Someone is going to have to explain to me someday how we called one a recession and one a depression. For example, in 2008, there was more than a 10 percent drop in the stock market, and I have seen definitions of depression as a 10% or more drop in the stock market. I also know a lot of people who are still depressed as a result of the Great Recession of 2008.) People today are still being served eviction notices for houses they never owned. There have also been stories whereby people have been evicted although their mortgages were not delinquent. This is America. We can and must do better.

In 2010, we all watched millions of barrels of oil spew into the Gulf of Mexico. The number of barrels ranged anywhere from 5,000 barrels per day to 80,000 barrels per day. It is interesting to note the lower the number of barrels spilled per day, the lower the fines that had to be paid. So in this case, as in so many other cases, if we change certain information to our advantage, we can change our bank account balances. Sadly, many empowered to manage information are improving their lives at the costs of many of the rest of us.

For many individuals and organizations this discussion may be too little too late. However, I am confident that the ingenuity and determination of the American people will meet this challenge for the benefit of us all and for the benefit of future generations.

But who will address this Imperative?

Information technology organizations over the last thirty years have proven that they are not able to improve information integrity, or simply believe that the integrity of the information is not their responsibility. Large audit firms were given the responsibility for ensuring the integrity of our financial information in publicly owned businesses, and yet in October of 2001, Enron suffered an Information Integrity Implosion causing catastrophic losses. Remember, no one stole the data. They did try to destroy the data that they had purposely manipulated for their own gain at the expense of their employees and stockholders. The Federal government then stepped in and gave these same audit firms the Sarbanes-Oxley Act of 2002, which created billions of dollars in consulting fees for these firms to again ensure the integrity of our financial information, and then the Great Recession of 2008 occurred. One after another, the largest bankruptcies in American history seemed to occur with each passing week. So how did these large financial disruptions occur within less than ten years of each other with all of this technology and government regulation in place? In this highly connected world, given most any circumstance, it should be easy to obtain what the facts are in order to take an appropriate action for that given situation. However, we now live in a time where we are engulfed with data, opinion, innuendo, misinformation, or plain deceit (disinformation).

How can we accept this reality and expect our quality of life, or even our mere existence to continue?

The simple truth is we can't, and the current reality regarding *information integrity* is unacceptable and unsustainable. If basic business and government information is fraught with integrity issues, how can any financial information that is rendered to demonstrate the financial standing of a business or the government have integrity?

Highly distributed, disjointed, needlessly redundant and overly expensive technology systems that currently exist throughout all of business and government have eroded our *information integrity*. It has clouded our decision- making and often hampers our productivity while in the process costing trillions of dollars and thousands of lives. Our confidence in American institutions has also been severely weakened as a result of so little *information integrity* both personal and public. At the heart of our national challenge, the real question is:

How do we not only improve information transparency, but increase *information integrity*?

But, again, who will do this? The lack of *information integrity* is costing Americans more than the US government has spent on corporate bailouts. It is my belief that the digital citizens living in the digital age must get more involved. We must understand what is really going on with all these databases that contain information about our money, our health, our purchases, our hobbies, our properties, and our identities. Our failure to gain the necessary insight to increase the integrity of our information will have undesirable consequences for generations to come.

Conclusion of Introduction

In summary, the Delusional Technology Syndrome (Chapter 1) has facilitated the manifestation of Digital Data Disorders (Chapter 2) that are impacting our lives in very negative ways and thus driving the need for an Information Integrity Imperative for the twenty first century (Chapter 3). There is a new way forward and a new day to prosper that I will cover in the Road to Recovery (Chapter 4). I hope you will gain insight from reading this book and will share your insights with others. I am also confident we the people will establish the appropriate levels of commitment to ensure the information stored and manipulated in thousands of technology systems, that have a high degree of control over the quality of our lives, represent reality in a truthful and fair way.

We have not lost our trust in America, nor our form of government, nor our way of life. Maybe we have lost trust in most corporations and politicians who avoid transparency. However, we have not lost trust in the American people, who created the most innovative nation on the face of the planet. I am certain the American people will meet the challenge of **Data Integrity** and make our nation and the world an even better place for all the digital citizens living in the digital age.

Chapter 1 - The Causes:

DELUSIONAL TECHNOLOGY SYNDROME (DTS)

DEFINITION: *DELUSIONAL TECHNOLOGY Syndrome (DTS)* - A symptomatic condition whereby the focus on technology is so intense that every business opportunity is pursued through technology and there is very little regard to what information is required to take advantage of the business opportunity.

Focusing on the Technology and Not the Information

Focusing on the technology and not the information can be compared to the dangerous allure of the Siren's Song. *Technology, technology, we have the technology you need, come and buy it. It will cure all your problems and make you rich.*

In essence, why do we keep buying the equivalent of a new luxurious Mercedes or a speedy Porsche to carry our garbage data?

We have over-inflated IT budgets, but why not the information we need?

There is a predominate thinking in many organizations that are inflicted with DTS that all we need is faster hardware or better software to make any situation better. Our focus on the technology is so intense that every problem looks like a nail and all we need is a bigger, faster hammer. Amazingly enough, the dysfunction of not having reliable information has become the norm, and these organizations are rapidly changing to the latest and greatest technology as a normal course of action without regard to what the business problem is and how best to solve it. In fact, there is very little or even no time and energy spent on defining what information is required. The technologists are much too intelligent to ask the business people what they need. Even more amazing in DTS organizations is the business people have come to accept this reality as the way things work and rely heavily on spreadsheets and other work-a-rounds to accomplish their work.

I once consulted with a billion-dollar organization that was changing out Sun servers for HP servers. This changing of servers was going to provision solutions for all kinds of business problems with the same applications and databases just converted to the new hardware. Not!

When we build multi-million dollar buildings, we usually have an architectural model that conveys the concept of the building. Engineers of different kinds then get involved and determine how the building will be constructed and with what materials. Finally, construction people get involved and the task of building begins and is carefully monitored by the architects, engineers, and government inspectors to ensure the building meets all standards for the safety of its inhabitants. If we build a $100,000 single-family home, the process is virtually the same as the process to build a multi-million dollar building.

In DTS organizations, we start with construction tasks by the programmers. They determine the size and type of computers, networks, printers, and software, and begin building screens and reports. In keeping with the building construction analogy, this would be like beginning to build a structure by starting with the roof and not involving any of those snooty architects or engineers. Any building has to begin with the foundation on which it is to be erected. Data is the foundation of any information system, and understanding and defining the data needed is where the process must begin if we are to increase information integrity in the twenty-first century. It should not start with technology, but unfortunately, it almost always does.

It should start by understanding the information requirements, which then drive the choices of the technology required. Interestingly enough, many DTS organizations already possess sufficient technology to fulfill their information needs if their needs were truly understood by the technology professionals. The business professionals should start with *raw material* (data) first. Second, develop an enriching *process* that transforms data into information. Third, the technology people should then develop *tools* (technology) to increase the *information yield* that will lead to more knowledge, which increases the quality of our life in the knowledge economy.

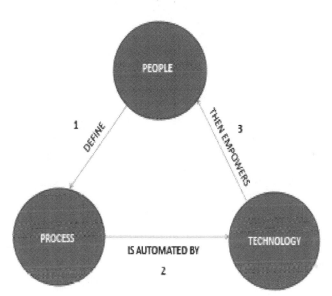

ALIGNING PEOPLE, PROCESS AND TECHNOLOGY

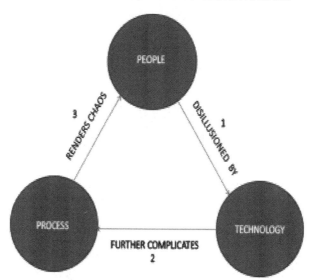

MISALIGNMENT OF PEOPLE, PROCESS AND TECHNOLOGY OVER TIME

The Arrogance of the Technology Professional

If only these people would focus on the information yield first as opposed to the technical solution, it would be a much better world in which to live.

Over my career, I have seen many intelligent people who work in IT departments. Their pay increased over time, and they were paid for what they knew. This created a highly competitive environment of who knew what when it came to technology. There is an old saying that goes, "Tell me how you pay people, and I will tell you what they do". Over time, this has created a large contingent of people who are self-centered, arrogant, and completely full of themselves because of what they may be able to do with a computer. They earn high dollars that continue to reinforce their over inflated view of themselves. The industry refers to this as IT arrogance. The technology professionals believe they know exactly what the technical solution needs to be for every business opportunity. They think those business people really don't know what they want, so why bother asking them.

My dad was an excellent, maybe even world-class, crane operator, but his skill in operating a crane did not hamper his interpersonal skills to relate to people and understand their needs. Many of these arrogant technology professionals fail to realize that the business side of the house produces the dollars to pay them their often inflated salaries. Furthermore, the tools they are provisioning are not meeting the information need, and increased benefits are not being realized. (See previous discussion regarding how the focus should be on the information yield and not the tool.)

What is more heart-breaking is that these people think they know everything, and you will have a very difficult time trying to convince them their approach is flawed. It is said that, "It is impossible to teach someone something they think they already know". However, these individuals are out in force every day creating Digital Data Disorders that most certainly will negatively affect the quality of people's lives.

Stephen Covey, God rest his soul, would identify these people as the "unconscious incompetents" - meaning they don't know what they don't know. But again, these "boys with toys" are much too clever to learn something different than their self-absorbed, cynical, and flawed view of how to provision a tool for an information need. A Significant Emotional Event (SEE) is looming in their future, which is typically the only circumstance that awakens an "unconscious incompetent."

The standard needs to become business professionals working with data architects and business process engineers to define the information need in order for us to do away with past practices. If left unchecked, DTS will continue to produce technology systems that will most assuredly create Digital Data Disorders that deteriorate our way of life.

The Shortage of Skilled Information Professionals

Information professionals ("I" professionals) working within the business must define the information need and be able to clearly communicate what the need is and why it is so important to the technology professional.

The technology professionals are not totally responsible for DTS and the Digital Data Disorders that are created as a result of our focus on technology. Business professionals have to develop information asset management skills that go way beyond creating a spreadsheet that can produce the boss's report.

Skilled information professionals need to develop the skills to define the meaning of the data, to label the data with descriptive labels that indicate the precise meaning of the data. Poor data definitions and data labels that are not indicative of what the data means are the symptoms of one of the most common Digital Data

Disorders. Additionally, the information professional must know what data exists and where it exists. They must understand the effects if the data is already available in another system and the costs and unintended consequences of recreating it. One of the Digital Data Disorders we will be speaking to in Chapter 2 are the detriments of having the same data being managed and manipulated in multiple systems at the same time.

The information professional has to be a responsible steward of the intellectual assets of the organization. The essence of information engineering disciplines dictate data becomes information when it has rich semantic definition, appropriately labeled and organized. So the Information Integrity Imperative of the twenty first century requires the rise of the information professional working closely with the technology professionals to determine the information needs before provisioning the technology. As we discussed in the building analogy, data must also be architected, engineered and then constructed if our information systems are to contain reliable, useful, and accurate information.

With this new role of the information professional, new organizational structures and responsibilities will need to be developed. As an example, if the information is found in multiple places in the organization, which "I" professional will have responsibility? What if the same information managed in different departments has different labels; what label should be used? Who provides definition to the data? These questions open up a valuable conversation in regard to the organizations who are embracing the Information Integrity Imperative.

Today, there is much discussion about master data management, big data, data analytics, and several other hot topics that the technology vendors are pushing us to buy. The discussion contained in this book is not about another panacea in the form of a new tool.

This discussion is about a cultural change that focuses on increasing the yield of information with high levels of integrity so we can increase our knowledge base and thus improve the quality of our lives. (Beware of the technology vendor's siren.)

Spreadsheets are Not Information System Solutions

"Beware of geeks bearing formulas."
Warren Buffet

I have constantly been amazed at what some people can and will do with a spreadsheet. I have seen some of the most valuable information assets of an organization contained within someone's spreadsheet that is completely unprotected. I worked with a fairly large retailer where I discovered millions of spreadsheets and hundreds of thousands of databases containing all sorts of the most sensitive data on desktops. With the release of MS Office 2010, Microsoft markets spreadsheet capabilities that can contain a billion rows within one spreadsheet.

When I learned of this new capability, it further encouraged me to write on the topic of information integrity. One of the principles we will cover in Chapter 2 is "that as the number of places the same data is redundantly stored increases, the information integrity of that information decreases." This principle comes about as a result of the increased complexity of synchronizing the data every time an instance of the data is created, updated, or deleted. For the data to maintain its integrity, the creation, update, and deletion of an instance of the data must be done in every location where the data resides.

One can understand the complexity of trying to synchronize hundreds of thousands of data storage locations every time the data changes, but this is exactly what doesn't happen across America every day. This leads CEO's to ask the question, which of the hundreds of spreadsheets has our accurate sales numbers this month? I have had CEO's ask me why it is that their marketing team has one set of sales numbers, the sales team has a different set of sales numbers, and then the accounting team comes in with yet another set of sales numbers. I always have to ask, "Which one do you believe has the real sales numbers?" Very rarely do I get an answer, but "Not to worry; it is only our sales numbers."

If they are particularly arrogant and full of themselves, I sometimes ask how they look in black and white stripes. Do stripes fit your color-wheel? New laws require the CEO to sign off on the accuracy of sales numbers for publicly traded companies or face imprisonment. Now which spreadsheet do we use to report our sales? I sometimes suggest chances are good the highest sales numbers will come from the group you compensate to increase sales. Who gets a bonus when we increase sales? Remember, "Tell me how you pay people and I will tell you what they do." Maybe the spreadsheet isn't such a good information system solution after all.

Definition: *Accountability* – Accountability can be defined as a full measure of willingness to sustain a value system. Accountability **is not** the willingness to change a measure and thus destroy the value system in the process.

People who build and propagate a culture of DTS will eventually destroy the value system which the organization is chartered to provide to its constituents. This will occur as a result of information values chains contained within every organization being tampered with to the point their measurement systems will no longer reflect reality. (Beware of geeks with spreadsheets.)

Business Leaders' Failure to Own the Information

If IT could only provide us with the data we need, we could make our numbers, our customers would be more satisfied, and we wouldn't have to work so hard.

This could be entirely true. This could also be the reason why so many business people have resorted to coping the best way they can. This may explain millions of spreadsheets and desktop databases found in most of our largest organizations across the globe. However, business leaders must not abdicate their responsibilities of holding support resources accountable for providing adequate levels of support, including their own information professionals. What I mean by this is business leaders have to define the information need and develop business processes that ensure the data maintains its integrity. Business leaders also need to be candid with technology leaders and forgo the passive-resistive behavior of saying everything is great. Even worse, if the business leaders and the technology leaders are involved in capital cronyism, then the culture they lead will be toxic and information professionals and accountants will perform the role of programmer and the organization will definitely be headed for a Significant Emotional Event in the near future.

It is time for the business leader dinosaurs to come up to speed with what technology can do for them and what information they need the technology to provide. I have had many conversations with business leaders who say, "We have a great strategy, but we just can't get IT to execute." If IT is not executing, then there is a part of the strategy that is not great and should be revisited. Usually, what I find is that IT is trying to solve "how" to accomplish something, and the question of what we are trying to accomplish hasn't been asked or answered. The information need that drives a desired business outcome has not been defined. Enter the need for the information professional to work with data architects and business process engineers to clearly define the information need before programming begins. And I will sometimes hear, "We don't have time to do it that way." To which I always respond, "If you don't have time to do it right, when will you ever have the time to do it over?" So if you must proceed with a limited understanding of the needed information, then be prepared to watch the business people break out their spreadsheets and try to cope with the low-quality, highly expensive technology systems resulting from the inability to employ sound information architecture and engineering principles.

In closing our discussion regarding DTS, all the facts suggest that DTS is the primary cause of low levels of information integrity. In the next chapter, we will move to the effects of DTS, which is the creation of four common Digital Data Disorders. These disorders are widespread and take a confusing situation to chaotic levels. As we discuss each one of these Digital Data Disorders,

I will share actual examples throughout my career where organizations have been adversely affected by the existence of these Digital Data Disorders, and often did not know they existed or how severely they were being impacted by their existence.

Chapter 2 - The Effects:

DIGITAL DATA DISORDERS

DEFINITION: *DIGITAL DATA DISORDER* **(DDD)** – A data condition whereby the integrity of the information is compromised as a result of a system error, human error, or human intention.

In Biblical terms, most organizations today would be related to "The Tower of Babel". The word *Babel* means confusion. As God had the Tower workers speak different languages, making their communications impossible, such is the interdepartmental communications within most organizations today because of Digital Data Disorders. We are basically speaking different languages.

The Tower workers weren't successful in building the Tower to heaven, and most organizations will no longer exist if they do not understand the existence of four Digital Data Disorders that are creating havoc. Many may wonder why we do not see these Digital Data Disorders if they are so detrimental. The symptoms of these Digital Data Disorders can be practically undetectable at first glance. Let me explain.

I have had two heart attacks in my life. In both instances, right up to the very point they occurred, I felt fine. How many people do we know who were walking around with cancer and did not even know it until something was found, like a small lump in one of their breasts? How many people today are enjoying that chocolate cake and not know they have diabetes? The point I am trying to make is these Digital Data Disorders can be present, and doing significant harm. Unfortunately, people, and the organization as a whole, may not be aware of the pending undesirable outcomes these

Digital Data Disorders are certainly going to lead to. Let us now turn our discussion to describing each of these four Digital Data Disorders and their detrimental effects.

What is Data Dyslexia?

Data Dyslexia is a data condition whereby multiple labels are used to identify pieces of information that have the same meaning, or one label is used for multiple pieces of information that have different meanings. In essence, homonyms and synonyms are extremely detrimental in high-quality information systems technologies. Remember, homonyms are words that are spelled the same and sound the same but have two different meanings. The word you see may not mean what you think it means. This data disorder is notorious for creating confusion as well as adversely affecting quality decision- making. An example could be the word STORE.

STORE can be a verb or a noun.

Homonym Example – I am going to STORE
(verb) my products in the warehouse and
not in the STORE (noun).

I once worked for a very large commercial bank that
used the word LOAN throughout their organization. It
was probably the most commonly used word in their
entire organization, and the word LOAN was used
throughout their technology systems. It was a homonym, which, again, is one word with multiple meanings. In the loan origination department, the term
LOAN referred to the concept of a credit line whereby
a customer could take multiple draws on their credit
line, if, for example, a customer was approved for a
credit line of ten million dollars.

Meanwhile, in the customer service department, the
bank had a different technology system, and the term

LOAN there referred to the concept of any *one* of the individual draws against the credit line of ten million dollars approved in the loan origination department. Let's say the amount of one of the LOANs in the customer service department was for one million dollars. The customer could take individual LOANs (draws) in the customer service department until the credit line limit was reached. In essence, the customer could take out ten LOANs, each for one million dollars, before reaching the credit line limit of ten million dollars.

So check this out. The customer would call the customer service department and ask, "What is my LOAN BALANCE?" The customer service representative would pull up one of the ten million dollar LOANs on the technology system, and communicate to the customer that one million dollars is the LOAN balance. The customer would say, "Great; I am going to wire you one million dollars to pay off this loan." The monies were wired and applied to the customer's LOAN, whereby the customer service department's technology system would then trigger a payoff via the corporate network to the loan originating department's technology system.

Well, you may have guessed by now that the loan originating department's technology system would then send the LOAN paid off papers to the customer for their LOAN of ten million dollars. YIKES! So a one-million-dollar payoff for a ten-million-dollar LOAN can be the undesirable outcome associated with one form of Data Dyslexia, in this specific circumstance.

The denial was very high with the people in the bank that this was a problem, because if you look at this scenario from the perspective within each department of the bank, no problem. However, given these corporate networks that we must have today, the data definition and data labels have to be harmonized across the entire organization. (Oh, wait, we now have network connections with our customers and our vendors, not just with each of the departments within our company. Hmmm?)

This type of Data Dyslexia literally took months to prove and ultimately resolve. But let's talk about the synonym type of Data Dyslexia. This one is most prevalent and is much easier to recognize but can be just as detrimental. A synonym is where two words are spelled differently and sound differently but have the same meaning.

> Synonym Example: "Can you tell me the opening and closing hours for STORE #432?" asks the customer. The customer service representative responds, "Sure. FACILITY #432 is open 9 a.m. to 5 p.m., Monday through Friday."

So in this case, STORE and FACILITY are synonyms. What is the big deal? What if the response the customer service representative provided was WAREHOUSE #432 as opposed to STORE #432, because FACILITY could be a reference to STORES <u>and</u> WAREHOUSES, not just a STORE listing? I once worked with a very large retailer that had many different ways to reference one of their STORES.

STORE_NBR, STORE_NO, STORE_NUMB, STORE_ID, FACILITY_NBR, FACILITY_ID, FAC_ID, FAC_NBR, LOCATION_ID, LOC_ID, LOC_NO...etc.

You may say this happens all the time. The challenge this creates is that every time a new STORE is opened, updated, or closed, every instance of where the STORE information resides has to be synchronized across all the various references of the STORE in all the various technology systems that references STORE. In essence, more coding, more testing, more disk space, more network bandwidth is required because we (programmers) decided to identify a STORE many different ways. You can bet that the law of unintended consequences comes into play because when all the references of STORE are not synchronized, we could possibly be sending customers to STORES that are no longer operating and are closed to doing business. Or we could be sending trucks loaded with products to an empty field where the STORE has yet to be built, but has been planned and has a STORE_ID, STORE_NBR, STORE_NO, or whatever the programmer decided to use in whatever technology system he or she was working on that day.

In conclusion, organizations that are inflicted with Data Dyslexia must embrace the Information Integrity Imperative and create a common language that has integrity so their customers, employees, vendors and technology can communicate and transact efficiently and effectively. Hopefully, you can begin to see how we label the data, and the definition we attach to that label, are of great importance. We will cover the remedy to both types of Data Dyslexia in the next chapter. But for now, let's learn about another one of these costly Digital Data Disorders that is also wreaking havoc in most organizations today, which I call Data Carcinoma.

What is Data Carcinoma?

Data Carcinoma is a condition whereby data is duplicated in many locations within the organization and is not managed in a coordinated manner. With today's technology, we can have the same data on our corporate server, our desktop, our phone, our drive in the cloud, and even in our paper files. Given the increased number of places we store the same data, the complexity of keeping it synchronized goes up exponentially. So one can conclude that as the number of different places we store the same data increases, the integrity of the data in all likelihood goes down. As a result of Data Carcinoma within a single organizational department, there are vastly different views on whose report actually reflects reality at this moment in time. This Digital Data Disorder not only creates confusion but can also create chaotic situations across different business units or departments whereby teamwork can be affected negatively. Additionally, customer interactions can be adversely affected and as a result, dilute the company brand.

Data Carcinoma is a serious data disorder that is spreading across the globe at a tremendous rate, as one might imagine given today's technological ability to duplicate data and transport it to many locations in nanoseconds. Data duplication does not have to be done in all cases, as we now have technologies to access data anywhere in the world it may reside.

So the classic example of Data Carcinoma is where an organization has customer data in their marketing technology system, their sales technology system, their manufacturing and distribution technology system and oh, yes, we have to bill the customer, so we must have customer data in our accounting and finance systems as well. Now the customer changes his or her address and the address change occurs in only one of the aforementioned technology systems. In fact, any customer information change now requires multiple technology systems having to be maintained or risk out of date information.

My favorite example of Data Carcinoma is when a cable company, phone company, or credit card company markets me as a new customer when I am already an existing customer. Oh, and to add insult to injury, because they have no clue that I am already a customer, their new customer offering is better than the one I have as an existing customer! Thanks a lot. A sure sign they do not value me as an existing customer is when their marketing department does not even know I am a customer.

Another example of Data Carcinoma occurred when I was working with a large retailer who had a marketing program for baby products. Parents could join the baby club and receive free gifts for their children on their child's birthday. Sadly, in this scenario, a child died and the parents received birthday greetings and free gifts after the child had passed. The parents notified the store to remove their child from the baby club and indicated their child had died and they no longer wanted to receive the gifts and greetings. Unfortunately, for the next couple of years, the parents continued to receive the gifts and greetings on their deceased child's birthday because although the marketing department had removed the child from their database, an outsourced fulfillment house had not. The parents pursued legal action and prevailed.

As I indicated earlier, Data Carcinoma can and does dilute the brand of an organization. Knowing what data we have and where that data resides is very important and can go a long way in treating Data Carcinoma. However, we will speak in detail to the prescription to cure Data Carcinoma in the next chapter.

We have now defined and given examples of two of the four Digital Data Disorders that have levied confusion and chaos on organizations across the globe. The consequences of these Digital Data Disorders can be, and have been, severe for many organizations and their customers. Data Dyslexia and Data Carcinoma, if left unchecked, will lead to the next Digital Data Disorder that I label and define as Data Atrophy.

What is Data Atrophy?

Data Atrophy is a condition characterized by a collective mistrust of the data. Because Data Dyslexia and Data Carcinoma have not been addressed, the integrity of the data continues to deteriorate. Often, an entire technology system is abandoned by its users because the data contained within the system is so unreliable and unusable. With this Digital Data Disorder, there is beginning to be a collective recognition within the organization that there is a widespread problem with the data and is beginning to affect the operation of the organization in very negative ways.

With the recognition of a widespread data problem, a DTS organization will begin the budgeting and building process of provisioning another technology system that in all likelihood will have the same inherent issues the existing technology system has. I have seen it time and time again, where organizations implementing new systems such as customer relationship management, enterprise resource planning, enterprise data warehousing, and many other major systems never focus on their current data condition to see if that may be the real issue. They will modernize every piece of technology but never think they need to modernize their information. If the data condition is the real issue, a new system with the same old data will not change anything for the better. (GIGO: Garbage data In means Garbage data Out.) Rarely do I see that the organization has created the definition of the information need driving the opportunity for a new multi-million-dollar system.

In recent years I believe we have moved from the communication economy to the knowledge economy within the Information Age. As a result, there seems to be more and more focus on an organization's desire for actionable intelligence. Business leaders are searching their technology systems to find the actionable intelligence to be able to increase revenue, contain costs, and improve customer satisfaction so that they may be able to achieve and sustain a competitive advantage. However, organizations afflicted with these Digital Data Disorders cannot turn their raw material (data) into high-quality information (yield). The continuum of Data-Information-Knowledge-Understanding-Intelligence will not be realized for many organizations that cannot turn data into information, and thus will be at a competitive disadvantage in the knowledge economy. They will lose the golf match on the first tee, so to speak. With increased pressure to compete more effectively with ever decreasing budgets and time frames, business leaders begin to cope with the total chaos the Digital Data Disorders have caused the best way that they can. This leads us to the fourth Digital Data Disorder, which I call Data Paranoia.

What is Data Paranoia?

Data Paranoia is a coping mechanism used by people in an organization who have taken matters into their own hands, and usually involves massive spreadsheets. They are managing their data in such a manner that it is not shared with the rest of the organization for fear of the data becoming corrupted. I was once working with a health care related organization where the president had Microsoft Access databases that he personally managed, to review certain customer's billing.

He had been embarrassed on so many occasions by billing inaccuracies that he developed his own coping solution to prevent the uncomfortable conversations of explaining away billing issues to his most valued customers. This condition can lead to even further deterioration of the data because more instances of Data Dyslexia and Data Carcinoma are often inherent with the creation of these self-made solutions, ultimately leading to a Significant Emotional Event (SEE).

What is a Significant Emotional Event? (SEE)

Definition: *Significant Emotional Event (SEE)* - A Significant Emotional Event is an unexpected circumstance that arises whereby the value system or the need system of an organization has to be reevaluated and improved immediately or suffer severe consequences. Failure to recognize the emergence of a SEE and take the appropriate action most often leads to other SEEs. Left unaddressed, eventually, an organization will experience an Information Integrity Implosion possibly resulting in Death by Data. Most organizations today that have thousands of spreadsheets and desktop databases are coping with the aforementioned Digital Data Disorders and may not realize the consequences ahead.

Spreadsheets used for limited scope analysis can be very beneficial. However, if these spreadsheets are used for business transaction processing or contain personal health information, financial transaction information, non-public information or the infamous credit card information, prepare for an unexpected circumstance to arise (SEE) that may involve the restatement of financials or the need to make embarrassing public disclosures of information breaches.

In summary, the intense focus on technology (DTS) has created the devastating effects of low-quality information (DDD). Left unchecked, DTS and DDD will destroy our way of life for ourselves, as well as future

generations. I have tried to define our existing circumstance with regard to data found in many of the technology systems that affect the quality of our lives, with
the thought in mind that there are remedies, solutions,
and better ways forward.

At this time, I would like to turn our attention from
Problem Definition to Problem Solving. Only by defining the right problem accurately do we have a chance
of solving that problem effectively. If one goes to the
doctor with a pain in their arm, there has been problem
identification (pain in the arm), but a trained physician
must determine the problem definition. Are we deal-
ing with a pulled muscle, heart attack, cancer, or some
other ailment? Treatment for cancer should not be
prescribed and applied to an individual with a pulled
muscle. So therefore, let's not allow our preconceived
notions of the technical solution to interfere with the
analysis required to define the problem accurately.

Because we can't really see or feel the data contained within the bowels of an information system, I have tried to use medical metaphors to increase awareness and to create a sense of urgency about the need to cure and prevent these Digital Data Disorders for the betterment of us all. So let us begin on a new path forward where we value our information on an equal footing with our wonderful technology, and by doing so, create a better tomorrow.

Chapter 3 - The Preventions:

INFORMATION INTEGRITY IMPERATIVE (III)

═══════════════════════════════

AS DIGITAL CITIZENS IN A DIGITAL SOCI-
ety, we, the people, have an unavoidable responsi-
bility to increase the integrity of our information to
preserve the wellness and wholeness of our way of
life in America.

Are you sailing on a "ship of fools" in the darkness of data or cruising on the "ship of dreams" with the illumination of information? A ship of fools will certainly crash upon the rocks they cannot SEE.

The Preventions of an Information Integrity Implosion

We need to recognize a Significant Emotional Event (SEE) when one occurs before we experience an Information Integrity Implosion, crippling or killing our organization. Institute an Information Integrity

Imperative and do not continue to be in denial of the negative effects of Digital Data Disorders caused by an entire nation gripped in a Delusional Technology Syndrome. The Information Integrity Imperative for your organization should address each one of the Digital Data Disorders you are currently experiencing.

There are preventions for each of the Digital Data Disorders that we will share in this chapter. These preventions will require the involvement of our "I" professionals, our "T" professionals, as well as the executive teams on the business and technical sides of the organization. The preventions will come in the form of techniques and not technology. There is no panacea. The culture of the organization has to evolve to be information yield driven, fact based, and not anecdotal in their decision-making. There is less and less room for error or rework in today's marketplace. Given, we are advocating a cultural evolution, the need for a robust change management program is required. The change management program needs to speak to at least the following plans:

Communication Plan: It is essential that we communicate the detriments of the status quo and the benefits of the future state. In doing so, we will make the emotional appeal, the fire in the belly if you will, required for any major worthwhile endeavor.

Education Plan: To create the future culture, we have to invest the time and money in training our people in the best new practices. People learn in at least three different ways. They are visual, auditory, or kinetic in nature, and I would suggest your instructional design consider all three for your Information Integrity Imperative.

Compensation Plan: We must reward our people who are making the efforts to adopt the best practices in their work lives. We also must decompensate those individuals who are holding onto detrimental practices of the past when it comes to information management in the second decade of the twenty-first century.

What is the Prevention for Data Dyslexia?

Instituting naming standards, abbreviation standards, and creating data definitions for all major data elements are required for the prevention of Data Dyslexia and are of primary importance. The naming standards need to be applied and governed in all major transaction and analysis information systems. The "I" professional assigned to a particular business area or business function must first assess the current state and begin to create an inventory of the intellectual assets found In their area of responsibility. The "I" professional should begin to analyze how their major data elements are labeled and what the definitions of these elements are. The business executives need to make the "I" professional assignments. Individuals assigned to their given area must create an information asset management group whereby each "I" professional can present their inventories and begin the process of establishing consistent naming, abbreviation, and definition standards.

What is the Prevention for Data Carcinoma?

Reusing versus recreating the data whenever and wherever possible is the best course of action to prevent Data Carcinoma. Chances are an organization that is suffering from Data Carcinoma is most likely not employing data modeling practices or distributed data architecture practices. Data modeling is a skill required for being an "I" professional in the twenty-first century. The enterprise data architect should be a "T" professional because of the technical skills required, and they should work very closely with all of the "I" professionals. Another major consideration in order for Data Carcinoma to be managed effectively is identifying the information system or service of record for each major data element. In our world of distributed computing, the same data may have to reside in multiple places, but should only be managed (created, updated, deleted) in one information system or service. Any changes to the data are then propagated to any other information systems where the same data may reside.

What is the Prevention for Data Atrophy?

The recognition that information is an indispensable enterprise strategic asset is required to prevent Data Atrophy. When an organization's data condition has progressed to Data Atrophy, an inspiring, visionary leader must come forth and declare an Information Integrity Imperative. The extent of the multi-faceted damages inflicted upon the corporate culture, and its capabilities, have to be fully determined and communicated to begin the required work of painting the rich vision of the future. This is the first and most important step of an information-driven culture that is empowered to turn raw data into high-quality information. If entire technology systems have been abandoned because of the unreliable nature of the data, the data condition within that organization has deteriorated to a dangerous point. The current leadership will be incapable of bringing about the required changes to prevent the onset of Significant Emotional Events soon to be arriving at the organization's front door.

At this major crossroad, the corporation as it currently exists, is in danger of experiencing an Information Integrity Implosion. I strongly encourage the President, CEO, and Board to take immediate action to find an experienced information professional to come in and lead an Information Integrity Imperative for your organization. When a corporation is experiencing the symptoms associated with Data Atrophy and/or Data Paranoia, the data condition has reached a crisis level! A new culture is required as quickly as possible given the presence of these Digital Data Disorders.

What is the Prevention for Data Paranoia?

An entire enterprise information asset management strategy is needed for the prevention of Data Paranoia. This involves realizing data is not just data, but is an indispensable strategic asset required for the organization to create and sustain competitive advantage in the twenty-first century. The inspired visionary leader required for Data Atrophy will come in and know that managing data as a competitive advantage will be the centerpiece of the Information Integrity Imperative, and that "T" professionals can no longer be left on their own to meet the information need.

Chapter 4 - The Road to Recovery:

CREATING AND SUSTAINING COMPETITIVE ADVANTAGE

"If you do not change direction, you may end up where you are heading." — Gautama Buddha

Yikes!!

Assess Your Current Data Condition

Assessing your current data condition is the first step on the Road to Recovery. Given the four Digital Data Disorders we covered in Chapter 2, can you relate to any of the symptoms that these disorders may be causing? Regarding Data Dyslexia, are there naming standards and coding standards in place that are governed by an information asset management group? Given the widespread nature of Data Carcinoma, do you have "I" professionals located in the business units who have responsibility for the intellectual assets in their business units and can identify the system or service of record for each major data element? Wide scale knowledge of data quality issues throughout the organization that are sometimes joked about or taken lightly is a classic symptom of Data Atrophy. And, finally, Data Paranoia the most serious disorder of an organization's data condition, is the use of desktop databases and spreadsheets that contain the organization's most sensitive and critical data.

Typically, conducting a data condition assessment can be accomplished within four to six weeks. This assessment should only determine which Digital Data Disorders are present within your organization. Once the data condition assessment is made, an Information Integrity Imperative for your organization should be created specifically to address the needs of your organization. Again, there is no silver bullet, and each organization's data condition is unique to that organization's culture and practices.

Separating the Winners from the Losers

It is a given living in the Information Age that information asset management has to be a core competency of every organization. However, unfortunately, not every organization values the yield of information, but instead values more the tool that manages the information. In our recent past, we have seen the largest retailer in the world, Sears, whose headquarters were located in the Sears Tower in downtown Chicago, overtaken by a small retailer headquartered in Benton, Arkansas. Many believe information technology played a key role in driving operating efficiencies that created a competitive advantage still enjoyed by Walmart today. Below is a competitive advantage matrix that shows Sears had a competitive advantage in every measurable way except in the area of information resources. Sears had a distinguished management team, the power of brand, incumbency, money and size. Sears possessed extensive distribution and physical resources as well as an offering capability that touted *"Sears has something for everyone."* And yet Sears lost their competitive advantage. Sears' roots were in the catalog business and failed to adapt to the changes in information technology. Today, there is a similar shift that organizations will have to make to stay competitive.

Organizations will have to shift their focus from Technical Resources to Information Resources if they are to remain relevant in the Knowledge Economy. The ability of an organization to maximize the information yield will be the deciding factor in the race to competitive advantage.

Competitive Advantage Matrix

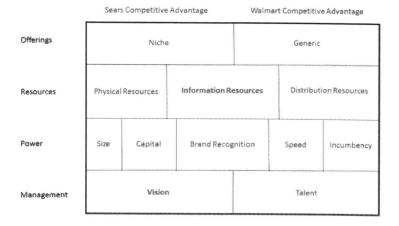

Conclusion: Strategic thought and action is required

Overcoming the Five D's of Death by Data

As in the Bible, the enemy uses doubt, delay, diversion, discouragement and defeat to prevent you from

enjoying everlasting life. I have seen these five elements keep an organization from moving forward to improve their overall data condition.

Doubt comes into play when an organization doubts the seriousness of their situation. They continue to want to focus on the tool and believe their ultimate success will be realized through technology in and of itself. Some organizations also doubt their abilities to improve the integrity of their information because of the amount of change required for the organization to improve their data condition.

Delay is often a tactic that is used to avoid knowing and therefore not having to confront the truth of their situation. Staying in denial will most certainly bring on Significant Emotional Events whereby the truth can no longer be denied. The harsh reality of not managing the integrity of their information will begin to be dealt with.

Diversion is an attempt to suggest there are other higher priorities the organization must address before confronting and resolving their information integrity issues. With each passing day, Digital Data Disorders left un-remediated only increase the volume and complexity of the work required to improve the overall condition of their information.

Discouragement will creep in when the overwhelming truth of the situation is becoming widely known throughout the organization. The feeling of "We will never be able to clean up all our data" will begin to be talked about in open forums. Large debates will break out regarding the practicality of trying to accomplish the goal of improving the integrity of their information. And finally, we don't have enough people or the right people to be able to accomplish our goal of improving information integrity.

Defeat will be spoken of when an organization makes multiple failed attempts at cleaning up their data. "We have already tried cleaning up our data, and we could not do it. We need to focus on more important things. Cleaning up our data is hopeless."

Establish an Information Integrity Imperative Today

An organization must adopt an Information Integrity Imperative, which is an unavoidable necessity in order to improve the integrity of information. This allows it to remain competitive in the knowledge economy. The Imperative must address the people, process, and technology aspects required to improve the integrity of their information. The people must be trained on information asset management fundamentals.

The processes must be defined and developed to perform the cleanup of existing data, as well as the ongoing processes to keep the integrity of the information at acceptable levels. There are also technologies that are available to help identify the Digital Data Disorders we have spoken about, as well as help remediate these disorders so that information yield can be fully realized.

Establish a collaborative group of business and technology professionals who will first assess the current condition of the organization's data. Identify and prioritize the Digital Data Disorders that require remediation to improve the integrity of the information in all major information systems throughout the enterprise.

Dedicate a group of professionals who will be charged with the mission to rectify each type of Digital Data Disorder we spoke of in Chapter 3: The Preventions.

Develop a testing and certification process that will be executed as each Digital Data Disorder is remediated.

A New Day to Prosper in the Knowledge Economy

Improving the American Economy for all Americans in America

The new competitive battle ground will be defined by what organizations will be able to take the raw materials of data and transform that raw material into information, knowledge, understanding, and intelligence, and those organizations that will remain trapped in a Delusional Technology Syndrome. Organizations armed with high information consciousness and high technology competence will be the organizations that will increase the integrity of their information yield, increasing their competitive advantage to the detriment of their competitors.

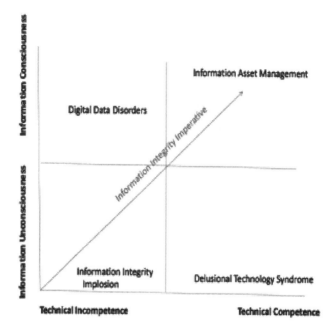

These organizations will declare and execute an Information Integrity Imperative that will provide them with the intellectual capital to increase revenues, maximize profits, provide outstanding customer service, and ensure compliance with all applicable laws and regulations. As a result of shifting their focus from the

tools to managing the information yield, these organizations will certainly prosper and improve the quality
of the lives of their employees and customers.

Godspeed to you and yours.

For more information, please see:

www.Dataintegritysolutionscorp.com